921
WHE

Moriarty, J. T.

Phillis Wheatley.

C3

$21.25

34880030029347

DATE			

BAKER & TAYLOR

PRIMARY SOURCES OF
FAMOUS PEOPLE IN AMERICAN HISTORY™

PHILLIS WHEATLEY

AFRICAN AMERICAN POET

J. T. MORIARTY

rosen central
Primary Source™

The Rosen Publishing Group, Inc., New York

Published in 2004 by The Rosen Publishing Group, Inc.
29 East 21st Street, New York, NY 10010

Library of Congress Cataloging-in-Publication Data

Moriarty, J.T.
Phillis Wheatley / by J.T. Moriarty.— 1st ed.
    v. cm. — (Primary sources of famous people in American history)
Includes bibliographical references (p.) and index.
Contents: Phillis's early years — Phillis writes poetry — Phillis is published — The end of Phillis's life — Timeline — Glossary.
ISBN 0-8239-4119-1 (lib. bdg.)
ISBN 0-8239-4191-4 (pbk.)
6-pack ISBN 0-8239-4318-6
1. Wheatley, Phillis, 1753–1784—Juvenile literature. 2. Poets, American—Colonial period, ca. 1600–1775—Biography—Juvenile literature. 3. African American women poets—Biography—Juvenile literature. 4. Slaves—United States—Biography—Juvenile literature. 5. African American poets—Biography—Juvenile literature. [1. Wheatley, Phillis, 1753–1784. 2. Poets, American. 3. Slaves. 4. African Americans—Biography. 5. Women—Biography.]
I. Title. II. Series.
PS866.W5Z626 2003
811'.1—dc21

                                                                    2003003810
Manufactured in the United States of America

Photo Credits: cover, pp. 10, 27 © Bettmann/Corbis; p. 5 The University of Florida, George A. Smathers Libraries; pp. 6, 26 Library of Congress Rare Book and Special Collections Division; pp. 7, 18 © Corbis; pp. 9, 23 © North Wind Picture Archives; p. 11 © SuperStock, Inc.; pp. 12, 21 Private Collection/Bridgeman Art Library; p. 13 courtesy of the Library Company of Philadelphia; p. 15 courtesy of the Massachusetts Historical Society; p. 16 Scottish National Portrait Gallery, Edinburgh, Scotland/Bridgeman Art Library; p. 17 Library of Congress, Manuscript Division; pp. 19, 29 courtesy of the Rare Books and Manuscripts Collection, The New York Public Library, Astor, Lenox, and Tilden Foundations; p. 20 courtesy of the Phelps Stokes Collection, Miriam and Ira D. Wallach Division of Art, Prints, and Photographs, The New York Public Library, Astor, Lenox, and Tilden Foundations; p. 25 Photographs and Prints Division, Schomburg Center for Research in Black Culture, The New York Public Library, Astor, Lenox, and Tilden Foundations.

Designer: Thomas Forget; Editor: Jill Jarnow; Photo Researcher: Rebecca Anguin-Cohen

CONTENTS

1 PHILLIS'S EARLY YEARS

It was 1761. White men sailed to Africa. They took African people from their homes. They would sell these people in the American colonies as slaves. They forced a girl about seven years old into a ship. It was packed with other African people who had been kidnapped. There were men and women, boys and girls.

DID YOU KNOW?
Phillis arrived in Boston on July 11, 1761.

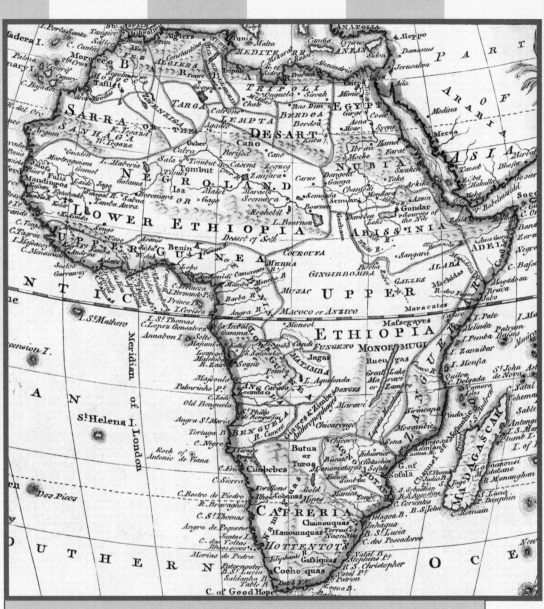

The slave ship that carried Phillis to Boston was returning from the west coast of Africa. This map of Africa was drawn in 1771.

The boat sailed across the Middle Passage. This was a route used by slave ships to travel from Africa to America.

The conditions on the ships were terrible. The Africans were tightly packed together. It was dark and hot. The African people wore heavy chains. They could not move very much. They didn't have much to eat or drink.

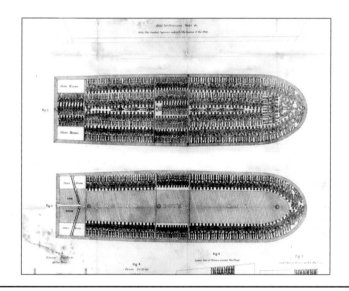

The trip from Africa on a slave ship took months. Many people got sick and died. Some people tried to kill themselves.

The artist called this 1855 engraving *Life and Death on the Ocean*. It shows African people imprisoned on a slave ship.

The ship finally reached Boston. The young girl was sold at a slave auction. She was very weak. All she wore was a piece of dirty carpet. She was missing two front teeth.

The Wheatley family bought her. They did not know her name. She could not tell them. She did not speak English. They named her Phillis. It was the name of the slave ship.

THE WHEATLEY CHILDREN

The Wheatley children were twins. Their names were Mary and Nathaniel.

TO BE SOLD by William Yeomans, (in Charles Town Merchant,) a parcel of good Plantation Slaves. Encouragement will be given by taking Rice in Payment, or any Time Credit, Security to be given if required There's likewise to be sold, very good Troopleg saddles and Furniture, choice Barbados and Boston Rum, also Cordial Waters and Limejuice, as well as a parcel of extraordinary Indian trading Goods, and many of other sorts suitable for the Season.

ILLUSTRATED ADVERTISEMENT, FROM THE "CHARLESTON GAZETTE," 1744.

The *Charleston Gazette* in South Carolina ran this ad for a slave sale in 1744.

9

Phillis was too sick to work hard in the house. But she was very smart. Mary Wheatley taught Phillis to speak English. She taught Phillis to read and write English, too. She also taught her to read Latin. Phillis worked very hard at her lessons. Soon she could read the Bible. Mrs. Wheatley was very happy to see Phillis learn so quickly.

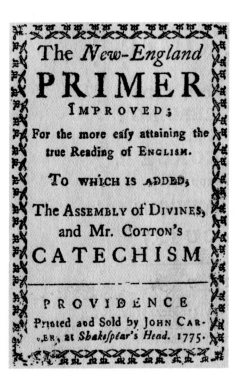

Phillis may have learned to read with a book like this.

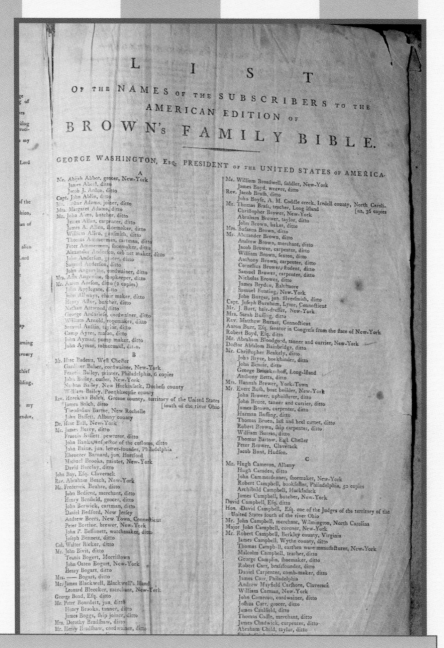

Reverend John Brown from Scotland wrote a Bible in plain English in 1778. It was published in America while Washington was president (1789–1793).

2 PHILLIS WRITES POETRY

Black people from Africa had a different culture from white people in America. Most white people in America didn't understand this. They thought that Africans were inferior. They treated African slaves like animals.

Many white people were impressed by Phillis. Because she could read and write, she was treated better than most slaves.

Phillis was best known for writing "On the Death of the Reverend George Whitefield. 1770." Reverend Whitefield *(left)* had wanted to start a school for free blacks.

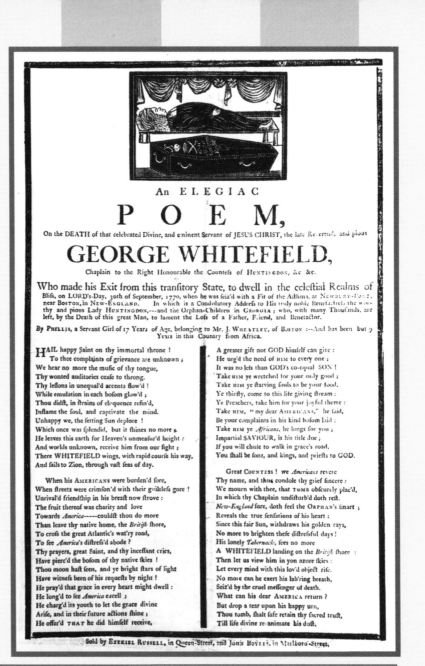

Phillis wrote a poem in memory of Reverend George Whitefield. She was about 17 years old. Published in newspapers in New England and Britain, it won her many fans.

Phillis soon began to write poetry. She wrote about religion. She wrote about people she met and things she saw. She wrote about famous people, like George Washington. Mrs. Wheatley liked her poetry. She encouraged Phillis to keep writing.

In some ways, the Wheatleys treated her like a member of the family. They were very proud of her. But she was still a slave.

FAMOUS PHILLIS

Many white people came to meet Phillis. To them, she was a living wonder. She was unusual to them because she was an African American who could read and write poetry.

Phillis Wheatley wrote this poem when she was about 14 years old. People in Boston were amazed by her talent as well as her beautiful handwriting.

An Address to the Atheist. By P Wheatley at the age of
14 years. — 1767
Muse! where shall I begin the spacious field
To tell what curses unbelief doth yield?
Thou who dost daily feel his hand, and rod
Darest thou deny the Essence of a God!
If there's no heav'n, ah! whither wilt thou go
Make thy Elysium in the Shades below?
If there's no God from whom did all things Spring
He made the greatest and minutest Thing
Angelic ranks no less his Power Display
Than the least mite scarce visible to Day
With vast astonishment my Soul is struck
Have Reasoning powers thy dark end breast forsook?
The Laws deep Graven by the hand of God.
Seal'd with Immanuels' all-redeeming blood:
This Second point thy folly dares deny
On thy devoted head for vengeance cry —
Turn then I pray thee from the dangerous road
Rise from the dust and seek the mighty God.
His is bright truth without a dark disguise
And his are wisdom's all beholding Eyes.
With labour'd snares our Adversary great
With holds from us the Kingdom and the seat.
Bliss weeping waits thee, in her Arms to fly
To her own regions of felicity —
Perhaps thy ignorance will ask us where?
Go to the Corner Stone he will declare.
Thy heart in unbelief will harden'd grow
Tho' much indulg'd in vicious pleasure now —
Thou tak'st unusual means: the path forbear
Unkind to others to thy self severe
Methinks I see the consequence thou'rt blind
Thy unbelief disturbs the peaceful Mind.

Many white people didn't believe Phillis could write poems. Most white people thought people with dark skin were not smart. Famous white people had written articles about black people. They said people with dark skin were a different species from white people.

David Hume was an important Scottish philosopher. He was one of the people who did not believe that Phillis could have written her own poetry.

the delay, and plead my excuse for the seeming, but not real neglect.

I thank you most sincerely for your polite notice of me, in the elegant Lines you enclosed; and however undeserving I may be of such encomium and panegyrick, the style and manner exhibit a striking proof of your great poetical Talents. In honour of which, and as a tribute justly due to you, I would have published the Poem, had I not been apprehensive, that, while I only meant to give the World this new instance of your genius, I might have incurred the imputation of Vanity. This and nothing else, determined me not to give it place in the public Prints.

If you should ever come to Cambridge, or near Head Quarters, I shall be happy to see a person so favoured by the Muses, and to whom nature has been so liberal and beneficent in her dispensations.

I am, with great Respect,
Your obed't humble servant,
G. Washington.

No. 7. To the Hon'ble Landon Carter Esqr. Virg'a.

Cambridge. March 25th 1776.

Dear Sir,

I have been honoured with your favour of the 20th Ultimo, and although I might intrench myself be-

---

Phillis sent George Washington a poem she had written about him. He replied with this letter of thanks on February 28, 1776. Praising her talent, he invited her to visit him.

Mr. Wheatley wanted to prove that Phillis was very smart. He wanted to show the world that she had written her own poems.

He arranged for a group of men in Boston to question Phillis. They included the governor of Massachusetts, John Hancock, and church leaders. They decided that her intelligence was real.

Nearly all of the men who tested Phillis to see if she was really smart owned slaves. One of the men was John Hancock *(left)*.

The following is a Copy of a LETTER *sent by the Author's Master to the Publisher.*

PHILLIS was brought from *Africa* to *America*, in the year 1761, between seven and eight years of age. Without any assistance from school education, and by only what she was taught in the family, she, in sixteen months time from her arrival, attained the English Language, to which she was an utter stranger before, to such a degree, as to read any, the most difficult parts, of the sacred writings, to the great astonishment of all who heard her.

As to her WRITING, her own curiosity led her to it; and this she learnt in so short a time, that in the year 1765, she wrote a Letter to the Rev. Mr. OC: COM, the *Indian* minister, while in *England*.

She has a great inclination to learn the Latin tongue, and has made some progress in it. This relation is given by her Master who bought her, and with whom she now lives.

JOHN WHEATLEY.

Boston, November 14, 1772.

John Wheatley wrote an introduction to Phillis's book. He wanted people to know that she had really written her own poems. At the time, many people did not believe that Africans could learn to read and write.

19

At that time, Massachusetts was a British colony. Many colonists were unhappy with British rules. They did not want to pay taxes to Great Britain for tea and other things. These colonists were ready to fight for freedom from Britain. The American Revolution was coming. Phillis would see what was happening from her home in Boston.

Phillis would have heard all about the Boston Tea Party. It took place near where she lived in 1773.

The Battle of Bunker Hill took place near Boston in 1775. It was the first major battle of the Revolutionary War. It proved that Americans could put up a good fight against the British.

3 PHILLIS IS PUBLISHED

Phillis wrote many poems. Mrs. Wheatley had arranged for them to be published. Phillis wrote a book. No one in Boston would publish it because it was written by a slave.

The Wheatleys sent a copy of Phillis's book to London. Archibald Bell agreed to publish it there. It would have a picture of Phillis on the front. People would know she was black.

DID YOU KNOW?

It is believed that the slave Scipio Moorhead drew the portrait of Phillis for her book.

Phillis Wheatley's portrait appeared on the cover of her book. Published in 1773, it was the first book of poetry written by an African American.

Phillis's book was being published in London. She and Mr. Wheatley sailed there. The sea air was good for her asthma.

Phillis met many celebrities in London. Even King George wanted to meet her.

When Phillis and Mr. Wheatley returned to Boston, the Wheatleys freed her. She was no longer a slave!

WOMEN POETS IN AMERICA

Anne Bradstreet was the first American woman poet to be published. Phillis was the second.

This is a rare picture of Phillis Wheatley dressed in a gown and jewels. It appeared in a French magazine between 1834 and 1842.

4 THE END OF PHILLIS'S LIFE

The Wheatleys helped Phillis a lot. But within a few years they had all died.

John Peters was another freed slave. Phillis married him in 1778. John struggled to make ends meet. They sank into terrible poverty. Phillis's three children died. John abandoned her. Some historians think he went to debtor's prison.

Phillis wrote a lot of letters. We know a lot about her because many people saved these letters.

In the 1700s, people who could not pay their bills were sent to debtor's prison. This is what a prison looked like in 1809.

Phillis became very poor. She could not sell another book.

She died in 1784, at the age of thirty-one. Nobody knows for sure where she is buried.

Fifty years later, Margaretta Odell wrote a book about Phillis. It was very sad. Being black in a white society took its toll. Phillis was brave. We should remember her struggle.

BIG TREASURE!

In 1998 a poem called "Ocean" by Phillis Wheatley was discovered in an attic. It sold for almost $70,000.

MARRIED, at her Father's Mansion, in Dux-
bury, by the Rev. Mr. Sanger, the amiable Mifs
NABBY ALDEN, youngeft Daughter of Colonel
Briggs Alden, of that Place, to Mr. BEZA HAY-
WARD, of Bridgewater.

Laft Lord's day died, Mrs. PHILLIS
PETERS, (formerly Phillis Wheatly)
aged 31, known to the literary world by
her celebrated mifcellaneous Poems. Her
funeral is to be this afternoon, at 4 o'clock,
from the houfe lately improved by Mr.
Todd, nearly oppofite Dr. Bulfinch's, at
Weft-Bofton, where her friends and ac-
quaintance are defired to attend.

NAVAL-OFFICE, Bofton, December 9.
        E N T E R E D.
Brig Harriet,   Sturgifs,   New-York.
_____ Independence, Lonol,   Martinico.
Sloop Sally & Polly, Sturgifs, New-York.
_____ Ruby,   Godfrey,   N. Carolina.

Phillis died on December 5, 1784. Her obituary ran in *The
Massachusetts Spy*. Published by an American patriot, it was
one of the few papers to note her death.

TIMELINE

1761—Phillis Wheatley arrives in Boston from West Africa. She is sold as a slave to the Wheatley family.

1767—Phillis's first poem is published.

1771—Phillis joins Boston's Old South Church.

1773—Phillis is freed by the Wheatleys. The Boston Tea Party happens. Phillis's book of poetry is published. It is the first book of poetry written by an African American.

1774—Mrs. Wheatley dies.

1778—Mr. Wheatley and Mary Wheatley die. Phillis marries John Peters.

1784—Phillis Wheatley dies.

1786—Phillis's book is first printed in America.

GLOSSARY

abandon (uh-BAN-dun) To leave without planning to come back.

celebrated (SEH-luh-BRAY-ted) Being treated as special.

cramped (KRAMPT) Being packed tightly.

culture (KUL-chur) The beliefs, practices, art, and faiths of a group of people.

debtor (DEH-tur) One who owes.

historian (hih-STOR-ee-un) Someone who studies the past.

kidnapped (KID-napt) Having been carried off by force.

memoir (MEM-wahr) A report of a personal experience.

publication (PUB-lih-KAY-shun) The production of a book or magazine so people can read it.

society (soh-SY-ih-tee) A group of people with similar traditions, activities, and institutions.

WEB SITES

Due to the changing nature of Internet links, the Rosen Publishing Group, Inc., has developed an online list of Web sites related to the subject of this book. This site is updated regularly. Please use this link to access the list:

http://www.rosenlinks.com/fpah/.pwhe

PRIMARY SOURCE IMAGE LIST

Page 5: Map of Africa, by T. Cooke, 1771, engraved in color for *Drake's Voyages*, London, England.

Page 7: *Life and Death on the Ocean*, Henry Howe, engraved in 1855, courtesy of Corbis.

Page 9: Ad for slave auction placed by William Yeoman, 1744, *Charleston Gazette*, Charleston, South Carolina.

Page 10: *The New-England Primer IMPROVED*, 1775, printed and sold in Providence, Rhode Island, courtesy of Bettman/Corbis.

Page 11: *Brown's Family Bible*, American Edition, List of subscribers, first published in England in 1778, American Bible Society, New York.

Page 12: Painting of Reverend M. George Whitefield, Bridgeman Art Library.

Page 13: "On the Death of the Reverend George Whitefield," written by Phillis Wheatley, engraved in Boston, Massachusetts, Library of Congress, Washington, D.C.

Page 15: "An Address to the Atheist," written by Phillis Wheatley in her own hand, Massachusetts Historical Society.

Page 16: Portrait of David Hume, by Allan Ramsay, oil on canvas, 1766, Scottish National Portrait Gallery, Edinburgh, Scotland.

Page 17: Letter from George Washington, February 28, 1776, in his own hand, Manuscripts Division, Library of Congress, Washington, D.C.

INDEX

ABOUT THE AUTHOR

J.T. Moriarty, an Oberlin College graduate, studied art history and wrote criticism for *The Oberlin Review*. He now lives in New York City with two cats, a turtle, and a marmot.